Isaiah Kai Huff's

Captain I Visits The Hospital

ISBN: 978-1-64050-243-7
PCN: 2018947889

Printed in the United States Of America

DEDICATION

This book is dedicated to all the sick children of the world.

Thank you to my mom, Shanna and my dad, Steve for always helping me and encouraging me to do great things.

Thank you to my Pastor, Rev. Dr. Miriam Burnett for always helping me and showing me that I am special.

Thank you to my AME family; especially the Missionary Society, Sister Sylvia Lett and Miss. Earlene Gaskins for seeing my vision with "Isaiah Inspires" and donating to its cause.

Thank you to my family; especially my brothers and sister, my grandmother, my aunts, my god-mom and god-dad and cousins for supporting me when I am in and out of the hospital.

Thank you to all my family, friends and church family who believed in me and help me realize I can do anything I put my mind to.

Thank you to everyone who shares my inspirational videos on social media.

I love you all!

#IAMAME

"Sickle Strong All Day Long" is my motto!!

"I will continue to be an advocate for Sickle Cell Disease and help whomever I can one day at a time." – Isaiah Kai Huff

sickle cell anemia

CONTENTS

Inspiring Joey

It was a nice day outside, so Captain I and his friends decided to go take a little trip to the Children's Hospital.

Their first stop was the Sickle Cell Unit. Captain I was so excited to see how all the children were doing. He even brought "Isaiah Inspires" bags for each of them!

The moment Captain I arrived, he met a boy named Joey who has SS Sickle Cell. Joey's red blood cells are crescent-shaped, and they get trapped in small vessels and block blood from reaching different parts of his body just like Captain I. This causes pain and tissue damage.

As soon as Captain I walked into Joey's room, Joey's eyes lit up! Captain I handed him his bag and the first thing he pulled out was a PlayStation game; then the nurse brought in the mobile PlayStation, Captain I and Joey both shouted   with   joy!

Captain I and Joey played for a while and talked. Joey really enjoyed Captain I and his friends being there. Captain I, his friends, and Joey talked for a while about Sickle Cell and what he goes through because of it. Joey told Captain I that he will start sharing about his Sickle Cell and he really wants to help others who have it.

It was now time for Captain I and his friends to go visit the Cancer Unit. They said goodbye to Joey and told him everything will be okay. They even gave him a picture of he and his friends signed with all their autographs and told Joey they will visit him again soon.

Inspiring Nora

Off to the Cancer Unit they went and met a girl named Nora. Nora has Leukemia which means she has Cancer in her blood. Her immune blood cells are sick; they do not work properly, and they crowd out her healthy blood cells. Nora was sickly and weak because of a blood transfusion.

Captain I entered Nora's room singing "Happy Birthday" because she turned nine that day! Captain I's friends followed him in with birthday banners, a cake, presents and more!

Captain I read her a poem, "God is a pencil, Nora is a highlighter; God drew the world and Nora made it brighter"!

With that, they made their way to the Heart Unit.

Inspiring Taylor

At the Heart Unit, they met an eight-year-old girl named Taylor. Taylor's heart was not pumping enough blood to meet the needs of her body. Her heart kept pumping, but not like a healthy heart should. Taylor was having issues with her breathing that day and hadn't had lunch yet because she was too tired to eat.

Captain I and his friends went into Taylor's room and a huge smile lit up her face! She sat up in her bed and asked them to turn the light on. Taylor loves art, so Captain I and his friends set up an easel and canvas and they painted the afternoon away!

Taylor began to get hungry, so Captain I and his friends ate a late lunch with Taylor. She was so happy, and she said they made her day! Captain I said to her, "Don't worry about what tomorrow holds, live for today!" He gave her a hug, they took pictures and Captain I and his friends left and headed to the Children's Diabetes unit.

Inspiring Keshawn

Captain I and his friends visited Keshawn, a thirteen-year-old boy who suffers from Type 1 Juvenile Diabetes. He had been sick for a few days and didn't want to take his medicine or eat the right foods. He got very sick and had to be admitted to the hospital. Keshawn's pancreas does not produce enough insulin and causes high blood sugar in his body. He must take insulin every day and if he doesn't, he could damage his body badly. Captain I and his friends were sad to find out that Keshawn wanted to give up, so they entered his room with healthy snacks, salads, and fruit!

Keshawn was excited to see Captain I and asked if he had pizza for him. Captain I said "Nope!", today is

"Healthy Food Day" and we are going to enjoy afternoon fruits and veggies with you! Captain I's friends cut them all up and they played a game with Keshawn called, "Guess the Fruit".

They blindfolded Captain I and Keshawn, they had to take a piece of the fruit, taste it and tell Captain I's friends what the fruit was! By the end of the game, Keshawn and Captain I ate all the fruit and they all were laughing hysterically because Captain I thought that the green melon was cantaloupe!

Just then, Keshawn's nurse came in because it was time to take his insulin. Keshawn didn't want to and immediately became upset. Captain I stepped in and asked the nurse to show him how it is done. He wanted to learn so that he could coach Keshawn to do it himself. Before the nurse could respond, Keshawn stopped her and said, "I got this", and he showed Captain I the way he gives himself the insulin.

Captain I and his friends cheered him along! Keshawn felt happy that someone understood and cared about what he was going through! Captain I gave Keshawn his phone number and told him to call him every day when it was time for his medicine so that he could be right there with him. Keshawn agreed!

Captain I told Keshawn that it was very important that he ate healthy foods and drank lots of water. He left a salad with Keshawn and gave him a gift card to the produce store! Keshawn's eyes lit up!

Before Captain I left, they chanted, "I am healthy, I am strong, I am a trooper all day long!" Captain I and his friends left Keshawn and headed to the Children's Lupus Unit.

Inspiring Tamara

When they got to the next unit, they met a girl named Tamara. She was eleven years old and suffered from Lupus.   Lupus causes inflammation in different parts of the body. Tamara has Systemic Lupus Erythematosus or SLE. She suffers from all types of problems including joint pain and fevers.   She was in the middle of a Lupus flare-up and needed to be in the hospital at the time.

Captain I knows exactly how it feels to have pain in his body and he wanted to make Tamara feel special. Just like Sickle Cell, there is no known cure for Lupus. Captain I gave Tamara a purple Lupus Warrior T-Shirt and provided her with heat packs, books, games, and puzzles. He also gave her a lesson on eating the right foods and staying hydrated.

Captain I knew that Tamara liked playing Candy Crush on her mother's cell phone, so Captain I gave her an Urban Toons Tablet with the Candy Crush game already installed!

Tamara was so happy! She had something to help her take her mind off her pain while she was in the hospital.

Inspiring the ER

Captain I and his friends felt so happy that they visited and helped so many children that day that they didn't want to stop there. So, before Captain I and his friends left the hospital, they stopped in the Emergency area where there were all types of children with all types of illnesses.

Captain I and his friends went around the ER giving out books, toys, and words of encouragement! They took pictures and gave out hugs! Even if the kids felt sick or down, they felt a little happier and better because Captain I was there, and they knew that he cared for each one of them!

WORDS OF ENCOURAGEMENT

Follow your Idk
...Leann's Idk
Angela Gray

Do your best
Isaiah
Love Nana

Congratulations!
I Sarah! Best
Wishes on the you
success of
Book!

Praise God for the
Things he has
done congrats
for you Cousin Marcia

NEVER QUIT
YOU STUMBLE GET BACK UP
WHAT HAPPENED YESTERDAY NO LONGER MATTERS
TODAYS ANOTHER DAY
STAY BACK ON TRACK AND YOUR CLOSER
TO YOUR DREAMS & Goals
YOU CAN
DO
IT

You are a inspiration
to many people. Proud
of you and continue
to be great Uncle George

Zay,
You still owe me
$25.00 Aunt
Rollie

Keep Up the Good Work Sport!
Lanette Owens-Toles

Keep Doing your Best
You will Succeed!
Chis

Good Luck!
T. WALKER

Good Luck
Bless to All us
well!

Congratulations!
Awesome Job!
I wait to read
Book!
cuzzin
Shara

IM so proud of you
Love Mommy

Zay,
Keep inspiring me+
everyone else! Best wishes!!
Tumeka

Isaiah
I Love you...

Dear Ka...

Isaiah...

There are a great number of children suffering from different types of illnesses and diseases that we may

28

know or may not know about. We should never be rude to someone because their head may be bald, they could be suffering from Cancer. We should never be rude to someone because their eyes may be yellow in color, they may be suffering from Sickle Cell. You never know what problems children and/or their parents are dealing with, so weshould make sure that we show love and the deepest compassion for sick children and their families. Captain I and friends promise to make the lives of all sick children better!

"Sickle Strong All Day Long"

Isaiah Inspires

ABOUT ISAIAH KAI HUFF

Isaiah is a uniquely inspiring nine-year-old young boy who is loved by all that meet him. Although Isaiah has been diagnosed with Sickle Cell Disease and has been hospitalized more than a dozen times, Isaiah has made the conscious choice to not let that keep him down. Isaiah has a deep passion for sick kids which led him to start an organization called, "Isaiah Inspires" right from his hospital bed. He walked around the children's wing and started feeling sorry for all the kids who were hospitalized because of sickness and disease. He started wondering how he could make them happy and feel better. This one purpose defining evening sparked his idea for a movement of donating books, toys and other items to St. Christopher's Hematology Clinic and the children's wing of Abington Hospital.

Isaiah is the Sickle Cell poster child for the Philadelphia region. He has participated in "Advocacy Day" in Harrisburg, attends and raises money for the Sickle Cell walk, hosts community events to raise awareness, and has hosted several blood drives that specifically focus on the Sickle Cell community. Isaiah has been labeled a game changer by KYW/CBS 3's Mrs. Cherri Gregg. He has received numerous awards from his State

Representative, the Sickle Cell Association, Sickle Cell 101 and the American Red Cross for his work in the community and for Sickle Cell advocacy.

Isaiah's newest project includes sewing surgical caps for the Children's Hospital. Isaiah came up with Captain I, his very first book because he desires to be a superhero that helps kids get through the pain and discomfort of their illnesses and disease.

It was a pleasure and very exciting to be part of this book. I wish my nephew well. It has been a long time since I have sat down and started working on art. Isaiah has inspired me to bring back the gift that God has blessed me with. Thank you, Isaiah and Shanna Huff, for your love and trusting in me.

Gewndolyn Huff Basketbill
Hussian's School of Arts and Design

The copy-edit for this book was performed by:

GET YOUR NEWLY WRITTEN BOOK, MANUSCRIPT, NEWSLETTER, FLYER, BLOG etc. PROOFREAD AND EDITED TODAY!

IT'S SIMPLE!

Email:
letshavealookatit@gmail.com

A Subsidiary of Divine Image Creations LLC.

Additional editing and application of all illustrations into the book was rendered by:

Kingdom Illustrations Graphic Marketing Firm

"The Solution to Your Graphic Marketing Needs"

Contact Information

kingdomillustrations2015@gnail.com

www.kigraphicsfirm.com

Facebook & Instagram: @kigraphicsfirm

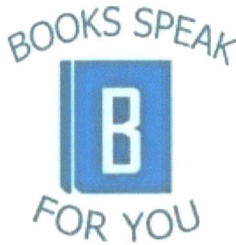

Published By
Pamela Denise Brown

Books Speak For You Children's Publishing

We Bring Your Stories To Life!!!

Specializing In 3, 7 & 21 Day Publishing
Publishing In Over 100 Languages
Printed In The United States
www.Booksspeakforyou.com
1-800-757-0598
OR
267-318-8933

www.ingramcontent.com/pod-product-compliance
Lightning Source LLC
Chambersburg PA
CBHW041808040426
42449CB00001B/12